KOREAN BUDDHISM

PLATE I
KIM KU HA, PRESIDENT OF BUDDHIST COMMITTEE
FOR 1917

[Page 35]

KOREAN BUDDHISM

HISTORY—CONDITION—ART

Three Lectures
BY
FREDERICK STARR

BOSTON
MARSHALL JONES COMPANY
1918

PRINTED BY
THE UNIVERSITY PRESS, CAMBRIDGE, U. S. A.

INTRODUCTION

THE author does not over-estimate the importance of this little book: it is nothing more than its title claims. It consists of three lectures given to popular audiences, with the accompaniment of many illustrations. It represents, however, a considerable amount of work in an almost virgin field. It has involved hard journeys to remote mountain monasteries, and days and nights of conversation and inquiry with many monks and priests. It is not, however, a profound study nor an exhaustive presentation. It barely touches many a subject, which would alone furnish more material than could be treated in three such lectures. It but scratches the surface.

The material which it presents is however new. Outside of Mrs. Bishop's account of her visit to the Diamond Mountain monasteries and scattered references in

her book to a few local temples, there is
almost nothing on the subject of Korean
Buddhism accessible to English readers.
A glance at our bibliography will show that
not one of the books or articles there listed
appeared in the West. All were printed
at Seoul, Shanghai and Tokyo and pub-
lications appearing at those centers are little
known outside. To aid serious readers,
who may care to secure them, the pub-
lishers' names are given in our list. The
author has carefully read all the items listed
and acknowledges indebtedness to all the
authors.

The actual amount of material for the
full study of Korean Buddhism is enormous. There are many voluminous works
in Chinese and Korean dealing with Korean history; when carefully sifted, these
will yield many important facts. Many,
perhaps all, of the monasteries have records of their history somewhat after the
nature of annals; most of these are in manuscript, but a few have been printed, presumably from wood-blocks cut at the establishment by the monks. There is a third

source of information, as vast in bulk as
either of the other two; it is the inscriptions
on monuments, which are scattered in thousands over the peninsula. The gleaning of
information from these three sources — for
the work must absolutely be of the nature
of gleaning — will require many years, but
the work is worth the doing. It is urgent
also. Every one of these three sources is
subject to destruction and even now is
threatened. Old books in Korea are being
constantly lost and destroyed; new editions
of them are often carelessly and inaccur-
ately reproduced; in some cases, the new
editions are intentionally mutilated, important passages being suppressed. The
monastery records are less secure than ever
before; with the new life and energy in
these old establishments, renovation and
clearing out of nooks and corners and over-
hauling of accumulations of papers, places
documents, the value of which is unknown
or unappreciated, in serious jeopardy. As
for the monuments many are disappearing
and others are becoming undecipherable
through weathering. There is pressing

need then of promptly securing these materials and making them available for study.

The Japanese are doing much good work. They are gathering old books and records. Up to 1915 more than one hundred and fifty thousand books, manuscript and printed, had been gathered by the Government-General. Among these were the "Annals of Yi" numbering sixteen hundred and thirty-three volumes and the "Royal Diaries," aggregating thirty-one hundred and ninety-nine volumes, "all hand-written with the brush." Of the "Annals" there were four sets made under the Korean government for the four old royal libraries. The "Royal Diaries" were compiled at the king's orders; they dated from Yi Tajo himself, but those up to near the end of the sixteenth century were burned by the Koreans at the time of the Hideyoshi invasion; those now existing cover the period from 1623 to 1907. Japanese scholars have organized a society for reprinting old and rare Korean books and have gotten out many volumes. They are piling up direct observations also. From 1909 to 1915, they conducted a peninsula-wide survey of ancient monuments and have printed the results in four fine volumes, with splendid illustrations, under the title *Chosen ko seki gafu.* They have taken steps toward the preservation and, where necessary, the reconstruction of important monuments and notable buildings. They are copying the monastery records and ultimately will have a complete set of all that remain. The originals ought to be left in possession of the monasteries themselves, with the obligation to guard and keep them safely. As to monumental inscriptions, the Government-General has been equally industrious. Up to March, 1915, there had been made thirteen hundred and seventy-seven direct rubbings from inscribed stones, of which forty-four represented Sylla, forty-three the period of the Koryu Dynasty and thirteen hundred and three the Yi Dynasty. It is fortunate that this preservation of material is being undertaken. The world will profit by it, though it may still be long locked up in Chinese characters.

In this book the work of Yi Nung Hwa is

mentioned. His Buddhist magazine should yield some data of value. If his History of Korean Buddhism is printed it ought to be of high importance, as he naturally has a much easier task in consulting the original sources than any foreigner. If his work is done with care and critical judgment it should be the necessary foundation for all future study. All depends upon how he performs his task. Readers who become interested in our lectures are advised to read Bishop Trollope's admirable *Introduction*. It clears the ground and indicates the direction of further studies.

The author has hundreds of negatives illustrating Korean Buddhism. One hundred and fifty pictures were used in the original lectures. When cutting down to what seemed the absolute limit, in selecting pictures for the book, he found that he had more than double the number permitted by the necessary conditions. Further reduction was difficult and many pictures have been rejected, which are more beautiful or interesting than some of those that are included. The final choice was based upon the desire to give as clear an idea as possible of actual conditions and to represent all the important phases presented in the lectures. One or two of the pictures were made by Manuel Gonzales in 1911; all the others are the work of Maebashi Hambei, who accompanied me, in my last three expeditions to Korea, as photographer.

Chicago, July 12, 1918.

CONTENTS

LIST OF ILLUSTRATIONS

[xvii]

LIST OF ILLUSTRATIONS

[xviii]

LIST OF ILLUSTRATIONS

[xix]

KOREAN BUDDHISM

KOREAN BUDDHISM

KOREAN BUDDHISM: HISTORY

SINCE 1911 it has been my privilege to make four journeys into Korea, so long known as "The Hermit Kingdom." To-day Korea has ceased to be an independent nation; she has been completely absorbed by Japan and forms part of the Japanese Empire. I found much of interest in the country. I studied the people and their daily life; I visited many of the famous points of interest and beauty; I have studied somewhat into Korean history. Nothing, however, has more interested me than the study of Korean religions, particularly Buddhism. When asked to give some public lectures this summer, I consented gladly to speak for three evenings on the subject of Korean Buddhism. My three lectures will deal with History — Condition — Art.

The history of Korea falls into three sharply marked periods. The first is known as the era of the Three Kingdoms — it ended with the year 918, a year easy to remember because exactly one thousand years ago. The second is the period of the Koryu Dynasty; it began with the year 918 and ended in 1392, a date easy for us to remember because precisely a century before the discovery of America by Columbus. The third period, known as the period of the Yi Dynasty, began with 1392 and continued until 1910, when the independent history of Korea ended with its absorption by Japan.

The history of Buddhism in Korea is divided into the same three periods, as the things which caused breaks in the national history were related to the religion. We shall then speak of the Buddhism of the Three Kingdoms, of the Koryu Dynasty and of the Yi Dynasty.

The early period is called the era of the Three Kingdoms because at that time the peninsula was occupied by three different nations. The largest, in the north, was

PLATE II

GENERAL VIEW: POMO-SA

called Koguryu. Japanese pronounce the name as Koma. It occupied more than half of the peninsula. Its capital city was P'yeng-Yang, still a city of importance. The second kingdom was smaller; in the southwest of the peninsula, it was known by the name of Pakche, which is pronounced by the Japanese Kudara. The third kingdom occupied the southeastern section of the peninsula. It was larger than Pakche, but smaller than Koguryu, and was called Silla, Japanese, Shiragi. Such then, were the three kingdoms which existed through a period of hundreds of years.

Unfortunately all names in Korea have several pronunciations. They are usually spelled with Chinese characters. If a Chinese pronounces the name, he will pronounce it in a certain way, dependent upon what part of China he comes from; a Korean will pronounce the same characters quite differently; a Japanese has still a different pronunciation. It is for this reason that the Korean and Japanese names of these kingdoms differ; the same characters are pronounced Koguryu by the

Koreans and Koma by the Japanese; Pakche on the Korean tongue becomes Kudara with the Japanese; and where the Korean says Silla, the Japanese says Shiragi.

Such then was the condition of the peninsula preceding 918. It was divided into three kingdoms, each with its own ruler. Buddhism, a religion which began in India, came to Korea by way of China. It naturally first reached the northern kingdom. It was introduced in 369 A.D. and its introduction was the result of foreign missionary effort. In those days there was an Empire of China, but there were also various small Chinese kingdoms along the northern border of the Korean peninsula. Buddhism came to Koguryu from one of these little Chinese kingdoms, the king of which sent its message by the hands of a priest named Sundo, who brought idols and sacred texts. He was well received on his appearance in P'yeng-Yang. The king of the country placed the crown prince in his care for education. In a few years the new religion had made

[4]

PLATE III

GENERAL VIEW: YUCHOM-SA, DIAMOND MOUNTAINS

[Page 35]

great headway. It had brought with it art and education, and the kingdom of Koguryu became a center of culture and advancement.

Five years later, in 374, another priest named Ado was sent from the same Chinese kingdom. His coming added impetus to the religion and two great monasteries were founded near P'yeng-Yang, over one of which Ado was placed, while Sundo had charge of the other. These two monasteries were not only centers of religion, they were full-fledged universities according to the ideas of the universities in those days.

After they were founded Buddhism continued to spread rapidly so that in 392 it became the official religion of the kingdom.

We are told that in the year 378, as the result of the coming of these foreign priests, the city of P'yeng-Yang was laid out as a great ship. To us this sounds strange. It is not easy for us to realize that a city was really regarded as a great ship and that a mast was erected in its midst, apparently in order that the sails of prosperity might waft the ship to good fortune and success.

Outside the city were stone posts to which the ship was to be tied up, and for many years it was forbidden to dig wells in the city because it was feared that if a well were dug, the boat would spring a leak and the whole place would be foundered. Such was science in the fourth century. It seems strange to us now, but ideas of that kind were rife in those days; in fact they have not yet disappeared from popular thought in Korea. I am not sure whether such ideas are connected with Buddhism, or whether they only form a part of that old geomantic philosophy which has so greatly influenced China, Korea and Japan through centuries. We find geomantic survivals of many kinds in many places. Old masts are scattered all over Korea, here and there, sometimes in quite inaccessible places; built of wood, they rise to a great height, and are sheathed with metal, which may bear an inscription and date. Many other places than P'yeng-Yang were thought of as great ships — temples, cities, entire valleys. (Plate VII.)

At Tongdo-sa, a great monastery in the

PLATE IV

SARI MONUMENTS: YUCHOM-SA

[Page 55]

south of Korea, my attention was called
to an iron ring fastened to a rock near the
trail. They told me that it was for the
tethering of a great ox, that all the mound
of earth and rock near there is considered
to be a great ox lying down; a hole about a
foot in diameter in the rock, close by the
trail, is said to be the nostril of the creature, and a knoll of earth near by formed
its head, while the great body stretched
out far beyond.

At Riri my attention was called to a
mountain ridge and I was told that it was
a running horse; two stone pillars stood on
the level ground near by — they were intended to prevent the horse from damaging
the fields. It seems that many years ago it
was realized that a running horse was
likely to do damage to growing crops; the
wise men of the district were called together and consulted; they determined that
they would destroy the danger by erecting
these pillars of stone, beyond which the
horse cannot go.

Perhaps ideas like these were taught in
those old universities in 375 A.D. Perhaps

they were then, as now, individual and professional knowledge, not to be learned in schools.

The new religion next entered the little kingdom of Pakche. This was in the year 384. This time it was not sent unsolicited by some little Chinese kingdom, but came by request from China proper. The people of Pakche knew what Buddhism had done for Koguryu and they asked the Emperor of China to send them a famous priest named Marananda. It seems that he was a Hindu, who had a great reputation for learning. He brought with him images and texts and all the paraphernalia necessary for the gorgeous ceremonials of his religion. He was received with great respect by the king and was lodged in the palace. Soon after ten other priests came from China and the religion made rapid headway through Pakche. It was from Pakche in the year 552 that Buddhism was sent for the first time into Japan. The king of Pakche sent images and texts and a letter to the Emperor, Kimmei, saying that it was a good religion, and that he hoped the Japanese would accept it.

Last of the three kingdoms to receive Buddhism was Silla, to which it came about 424. It is reported to have come from the capital city of Koguryu, P'yeng-Yang, and the priest who brought it was named Mukocha. He appears to have gone down the Taidong River to the sea and then around the peninsula and up the east coast in order to reach Silla. He is always spoken of as a black man, or negro; perhaps he was actually an African. There seems to have been some mystery about his arrival; it may be that the people did not like his color, or were afraid of his strange appearance. He hired himself out as a plowman to a farmer named Morei. His employer concealed him in a cave. It is said that when he was hidden in this cave it frequently shone with glory. Outside the cave there was a peach tree, which burst into bloom with flowers of five different colors, and in the winter, when there was snow on the mountains outside, irises and other flowers of wondrous fragrance are said to have broken their way up through the snow. The black monk is said to have worn a red cap and a crimson *kesa*. It would seem that the whole neighborhood must have known about these wonders.

About this time it is said that an ambassador from China came to the king of Silla at his capital city of Kyong Ju. The messenger brought various gifts, among them a substance which no one knew; it had never been seen before in Silla. It seems strange that the ambassador should not have known what he brought, but it is asserted that he was ignorant in the matter, and so the king sent to the cave — only ten miles away — and ordered the black monk to come to Kyong Ju to identify the gift. He had no trouble in recognizing it, because it was incense, common enough in Chinese Buddhism, but before unseen in Silla. He told them that when burned before an idol with prayers of faith, the god was sure to answer petitions. It happened at the moment that the king's daughter was ill, and he begged the black monk to try the efficacy of incense and prayer. Seven

PLATE V

MAIN TEMPLE: KUMSAN-SA

[Page 72]

days he spent in prayer before the idol and a cure was wrought. Soon afterwards Mukocha begged the king to send to China and the West for artists to come and cut figures in the rock walls of his cave, as he desired to make a chapel to the gods. The request was sent, the artists came, and it is said that they spent forty years in carving the wonderful figures which to this day adorn the walls of the little circular chapel in the mountain cave. It would require a separate lecture for me to tell you of my visit to that remarkable shrine, with its genuine treasures of art. (Plates VIII, IX.)

I must, however, say something about the old capital city of Kyong Ju. It had its period of glory, and its ruins are still impressive. Almost fifteen hundred years have passed since the black monk brought in the new religion. To-day there remains only a little town, but all the country around is sprinkled with the relics of the past. Here is the splendid grave of General Kim, twelve hundred years old. It is faced around with stone slabs, set firmly in place, twelve of them being carved with the animals of the

Eastern Zodiac. Here are the ruins of an ice-house, perhaps nine hundred years old; cunningly built of stone, under a mound of earth, with true arch-vaulting, it sheltered ice for the chilling of food and the cooling of drink a thousand years ago. There remains here a portion of a beautiful pagoda; much of it was destroyed in the sixteenth century, when Hideyoshi's army of invasion came from Japan and wrought havoc and destruction in Korea; built in the seventh century, it was a beautiful structure of splendid, thoroughly-baked black bricks and stone; stone doors below, moving on stone pivots set in stone sockets were decorated with carved work. To-day only the three lower stories remain, but they serve to show that the people were true artists. Here, too, one sees an astronomical observatory, built of stone, a sort of tower of circular form, seventeen feet through; it was intended for the observation of heavenly bodies; nearly thirteen hundred years of age, it is perhaps the oldest existing building constructed for such purposes in the world.

In those fine days, Kyong Ju was a center of trade and industry. Chinese, Koreans and Japanese were there; we are certain that Tibetans, Indians and Persians came thither, and it is claimed that merchants from Arabia used to stand in its market place. Of course we all know of the antiquity of culture around the Mediterranean Sea; we appreciate its achievements, and love to think of its glories; but we are apt to think of the Far East as being eternally stagnant and it surprises us to learn of a busy mart of trade in Kyong Ju, Silla.

And it had its scholars also. There was Ch'oe Chuen. He was a poet and essayist; he was a skilled caligrapher, writing the beautiful Chinese characters famously; he was reckoned as one of the great sages and learned men of his day in China proper, than which there was no higher honor.

During the period of the Three Kingdoms, Buddhism thus penetrated to every part of the peninsula. It prospered. Splendid temples were built, great monasteries constructed, magnificent bells cast, beautiful pagodas erected, figures carved by thousands. Religions that prosper too greatly become corrupt. State religions tend to become curses. Religious endowments tie up money which the people need. The dead hand may hold under restraint property which should be at work, helping the world. All this happened with Buddhism in Korea. In the last days of the Three Kingdoms Korean Buddhism was refined and artistic, impressive and beautiful, but was corrupt and harmful rather than helpful.

We may, perhaps, take the date 685 A.D. as marking the greatest glory of Silla. At that time she was gaining power over the neighboring kingdoms and before her glory ended she ruled the whole peninsula.

In 876 the king of Silla was named Chung—also called Hongang. During his rule the country was rapidly declining. He was followed by his brother, who in turn was succeeded by his sister, who became queen of Silla in 888. Her name was Man. The only reason why we mention these three rulers is that we wish to introduce the man who led up to the second period of Korean history. His name was Kun-ye. He was the son of king Chung, by a concubine, but never became king of Silla. When his aunt, queen Man, was ruling, he became a disturbing element, heading an insurrection. The glory of Silla was really past and the old kingdom was rapidly declining. Kun-ye was fortunate in having an excellent general, named Wang-on, and made headway with his rebellion; founding a new kingdom in central Korea, he gradually extended his rule, through the skilful leadership of Wang-on, until much of the middle part of the peninsula was under his control. But the man was mad, religiously mad. He was not only a Buddhist; he called himself a Buddha. Under the cloak of religion he did all kinds of wild and wicked things, and indulged in the most absurd extravagances. Finally the burden of his tyranny and his religious claims became so heavy that his officials plotted against him and begged his general, Wang-on, to dethrone him and seize the power. Ultimately that very thing happened, and in the year 918, one thousand years ago, Wang-on became the first king of a new dynasty, that of Koryu.

Before we leave the period of the Three Kingdoms, however, let us notice two interesting matters. You remember that Buddhism was brought to the Three Kingdoms by three priests — Sundo, Marananda, Mukocha. Sundo was a man from Tibet; I suppose he represented the great Mongolian race, that he was a yellow man; Marananda, who brought religion to Pakche was a Hindu; presumably he represented the Caucasic peoples; he may have been dark, but our courts would probably have to call him a white man; Mukocha was called a black man, a negro, and probably really represented the Ethiopian race. Is it not interesting that the peninsula of Korea should have received its first generally spread religion through representatives of the three great races of the world, the yellow, white and black? Buddhism, the first universal religion that the world ever saw, early made an appeal to all men, regardless of color and of race.

PLATE VI

SARI MONUMENT PYRAMID, KUMSAN-SA

(A relic of Buddha is supposed to be enshrined here)

[Page 72]

Two famous men, Chinese, lived during this period. Their names were Fa-hien and Hiouen-Tsiang. In 399 A.D. Fa-hien started on foot from China, to visit India, to learn of Buddhism and Buddha in the old home. He travelled many thousands of miles of weary pilgrimage in order to bring back with him fresh idols and correct texts and new inspiration from the cradle of the great religion. It was more than two hundred years later, in 629, that Hiouen-Tsiang made the same journey. Think of the danger these men passed through! They crossed deserts, which even to-day are almost impassable; they climbed difficult mountains and crossed broad rivers; they journeyed through countries of hostile peoples; they had to travel without artificial means of transportation through districts of foreign speech; they did all just to visit the old home of the Great Teacher, and to get his religion at first hand. We have the record of their travels. Their simple diaries have been translated into various languages of Asia and into English, French and other European tongues. Fa-hien was fifteen years upon his pilgrimage, Hiouen-Tsiang sixteen years. Both lived to come back to their homes to the great advantage of their co-religionists.

We have no diaries written by old Korean pilgrims, but we know that during the · glow of early convertship many from the peninsula made the same journey to the West.[1] Between 638 A.D. and 650 seven at least went from Korea to India to study the new religion in its old home. Most of them died there, never returning to their native land.

We now come to the second division of Korean history and its Buddhism, that of the Koryu Dynasty. You remember that General Wang-on, when his royal master went crazy and the officials revolted, seized the kingly power. He removed the capital to Songdo. Silla quickly went to its final fall and the new kingdom controlled the whole peninsula. Wang-on realized perfectly that the abuse of Buddhism had been the chief trouble with Kung-ye. His coming into power was largely due to an

PLATE VII
GEOMANTIC MAST: CHUNG-JU

[Page 6]

anti-Buddhistic movement. Still, he himself was Buddhist and while he did much
to check the abuses of the religion he continued to practise it on a more modest
scale. At his new capital he ended the first
year of his rule, 918, with a famous festival
of which we have a description.

There was an enormous lantern, hung about
with hundreds of others under a tent made of a
network of silken cords. Music was an important element. There were also representations of dragons, birds, elephants, horses, carts
and boats. Dancing was prominent and there
were in all a hundred forms of entertainment.
Each official wore the long, flowing sleeves,
and each carried the ivory memorandum tablets.
The king sat on a high platform and watched
the entertainment. (Hulbert.)

You see he was very far from cutting
loose from Buddhism. In reality, the religion flourished over the whole peninsula.
When Wang-on died in 942, he left a
written message for his son and successor.
It contained ten rules of conduct for his
guidance as king, which were numbered
from one to ten. Three had to do with
religion, and, of course, that religion was

Buddhism. In the first rule he advised his son to continue to recognize Buddhism as the state religion. The second rule was that he should build no more monasteries. While it was a good thing to continue Buddhism, it was a bad thing to build more monasteries, as too much money had already been expended upon them. The sixth of the rules was for the establishment of an annual Buddhist festival of the same nature as the one he had celebrated at the end of his first year. So Wang-on did not destroy Buddhism but continued it.

In course of time the old religion regained much of its harmful and destructive influence. From history we may cull a few events that illustrate its power. About the beginning of the eleventh century there came from China a fuller development of Confucianism than had before existed. About 1026 this influence became very strong; the official class, as was natural, was Confucianist; it organized and directed governmental action; between the officials, Confucianists, and the priests, Buddhists, there grew up a deadly conflict which lasted on through all the centuries. In 1036 the king was devoutly Buddhistic. He "decreed that if a man had four sons one of them must become a monk; because of the Buddhist canon against the spilling of blood, the death penalty was changed to banishment; another great annual festival was instituted. The king also encouraged the custom of having boys go about the streets with Buddhistic books on their backs from which the monks read aloud as they went along, to secure blessings for the people." (Hulbert.)

In 1046 it is said the king fed and lodged ten thousand monks in his palace. In 1056 or thereabouts one son out of three was compelled to become a monk. In 1136 it is said that thirty thousand monks were present at a single ceremony.

Under such circumstances, what would happen? When a religion had such a hold on the community—building splendid monasteries, erecting great temples, making idols into whose construction gilt of pure gold entered in quantity, making bells of metal that might have been better

used for practical ends, draining the people
of wealth by giving enormous properties
eternally into the possession of religious
establishments — a crash was bound to
come. It came in Korea. The country
had been drained; the people had been
heavily burdened; the men who as monks
and priests should have led in instruction
and good living were notorious examples
of profligacy and corruption.

At last, in 1392, a man arose who fought
against the king. The excuse for his fight-
ing was the fact that the government was
given over to a corrupt religion. Just as
before it was the successful general who
became the founder of a new dynasty; in
this case also he had been loyal at first to
the deposed king. The man's name was
Yi, and his title Tajo, and he is commonly
known in Korea as Yi-Tajo. He is revered
as the founder of the dynasty which has
just ended. In 1392 the old kingdom of
Korai disappeared and with it the dynasty
of Koryu, and in their place came the
modern Chosen and the Yi Dynasty. Seoul
became the new capital.

PLATE VIII
THE BUDDHA: CAVE TEMPLE, SUKKUL-AM

[Page 11]

Before we leave this period let me say something about *miriok* and printing-blocks. The word miriok has given me considerable trouble; I cannot learn whether it is a Korean or a Japanese word, or what was its first meaning, or whether it has anything to do with the word Miroku, the name of "the coming Buddha." Anyway the name miriok is applied in Korea to a stone that is worshipped; it is sometimes a natural stone and sometimes artificially shaped to more or less of the form of a Buddha. There are thousands of them in Korea. There are big miriok and little. My belief is that they were at first simple, natural stones, with something about their shape which was suggestive. They might be natural pinnacles, or rounded forms. Probably the old Koreans, long before the days of Buddhism, worshipped such stones and chiefly in order that the family might be increased. It was probably barren women and childless men who went to miriok and prayed for children. Then came Buddhism and took over the stone-worship of the olden time. Later

those miriok which were artificially shaped
to human form — Buddha-like — came into
being. Were there time, we would speak
of various of the larger miriok in Korea,
like the great pair at Paju and the couple
at Ansung. Of the largest, however, that
at Eunjin,[2] we will say something. There
are many strange stories connected with it.
It is apparently a natural pinnacle of rock,
which has been carved into the shape of a
Buddha; it is more than fifty feet high and
can be seen from a great distance; it is
more than nine hundred years old; in its
present form it is even to-day worshipped
by thousands of people; in the past there
have been times when tens of thousands
gathered at once to worship it. (Plate X.)

It is said that the stone suddenly appeared, pushing up from the ground and
that it cried out with the voice of a boy;
it was seen by a woman who was gathering
ferns for eating; when she reported the
miracle it was confirmed by an official
inspection after which orders were given
that it should be carved to its present
form.

PLATE IX
BODHISATTVA FIGURE, SUKKUL-AM

[Page 11]

No land surpasses Korea in its abundance of local tales. Every hill, valley, conspicuous rock, stream and pool of water has its story. Every miriok of prominence in the country has traditions associated with it. The one most commonly told of this great miriok runs as follows: A country man who had been to the capital, returning to his home passed this great stone figure. He noticed a pear tree growing from the head, which bore several fine pears. The thought occurred to him to carry one of these to his village as a present for the magistrate. With infinite difficulty he climbed up the smooth surface of the figure, — the magnitude of the achievement will be evident from an inspection of the picture. When he reached the face and climbed over the lips he hesitated as to whether to pass up through the nostril, — a foolish procedure as it was a blind passage, — or climb around the nose. He decided upon the former method and proceeded to worm his way into the opening. He experienced a mighty shock and, when he came to himself, found that he was lying on the ground. His presence in the nostril had irritated the figure which had sneezed, thus throwing him to the earth. Ruefully rubbing his bruises, he looked upward at the figure regretful for his lost effort. But he had after all been fortunate and the same sneeze which had dislodged him had shaken one of the pears from the tree and it had fallen on the grass near by. Picking it up he hastened on his way rejoicing.

The second item connected with this period to which I wish to refer is the cutting of wood-blocks for printing the entire Buddhist scriptures. The set of blocks is still preserved in the ancient monastery of Hain-sa. They were made during the reign of King Kojong and are seven hundred years old. There are eighty-one thousand of these blocks and each of them prints an entire page of a Buddhist text. Altogether they print six thousand eight hundred and five volumes, one thousand five hundred and eleven different works. A special building is devoted to their preservation and they have been taken over by

PLATE X

GREAT MIRIOK: EUNJIN. GENERAL VIEW

[Page 24]

the Japanese government as National
Treasure. (Plates XII, XIII.) The blocks
are said to represent the work of monks
through fifteen years and the set is reputed
the best in the world. Several years ago
Count General Terauchi ordered several
copies of the Tripitaka printed from these
blocks. One of these copies was presented
to the Emperor and a second is preserved
in the temple, Senyu-ji, Kyoto.

Yi-Tajo came to power through an anti-
Buddhist movement. Yet on the whole he
dealt leniently with the religion. He
crippled it but did not destroy it. Through
the greater part of the Yi Dynasty, however, Buddhism was at serious disadvan-
tage. Only for a short time under the king
Seijo did it have a momentary revival. He
ruled from 1456 to 1468. During his
reign a splendid temple was built in Seoul
of which we have an interesting contemporary description;[3] no sign of it remains
to-day, but the beautiful pagoda erected
at the same time, and the turtle-borne
monumental stone recording the occasion
of its construction are in existence in Pa-

goda Park at the center of the city.[4] This pious king was succeeded in 1469 by his young son, Chasan. His mother, the late king's widow, was at first his regent but in 1472 he took the actual reins of power and almost his first act was to drive Buddhism out of Seoul. He not only abolished all the monasteries and temples in the capital city, but in every city and town throughout the kingdom. The priests took refuge in the mountains and from that time down until these latter days there have been no Buddhist temples in Korean cities. There have only been monasteries in the mountains, often in inaccessible places.

Those were drastic measures and under them Korean Buddhism suffered and sank to lowest ebb. It passed through hard times during four hundred years and more of exile. Still the religion was not dead, and during this period of test it even showed some signs of worth.

In 1592, Hideyoshi sent his great army from Japan to conquer Korea. It was under two generals, one a Christian and the other a Buddhist. The invaders

PLATE XI

GROUP AT FUKOAN, BRANCH OF SINKEI-SA; DIAMOND MOUNTAINS

[Page 47]

wrought great destruction in the unfor-
tunate peninsula. Many of the temples
and monasteries in the mountains were
destroyed, altars were stripped of treasures,
monks and priests driven from their sanc-
tuaries. During this invasion some of the
priests showed themselves loyal, thus Hulbert tells us:

Hyu-Chung, known throughout the Eight
Provinces as the great teacher of Sosan, was
a man of great natural ability as well as of
great learning. His pupils were numbered by
thousands and were found in every province.
He called together two thousand of them and
appeared before the king at Euiju and said:
"We are of the common people, but we are
all the king's servants and two thousand of us
have come to die for Your Majesty." The
king was much pleased by this demonstration of
loyalty and made Hyu-Chung a Priest-General
and told him to go into camp at Pop-Heung
Monastery. He did so, and from that point
sent out a call to all the monasteries in the land.
In Chulla province was a warrior-monk, Ch'oe-
Yung and at Diamond Mountain another named
Yu-Chung. These came with over a thousand
followers and went into camp a few miles to
the East of P'yeng-Yang. They had no in-

tention of engaging in actual battle, but they acted as spies, took charge of the commissariat and made themselves generally useful. During battle they stood behind the troops and shouted encouragement. Yu-Chung, trusting to his priestly garb, went into P'yeng-Yang to see the Japanese generals.

Thus we see, that notwithstanding the condition of poverty, ignorance and unimportance to which the Buddhist monks had sunk there were still among them teachers of great learning with crowds of students, who were ready to serve their king in his hour of trial.

In 1660 a curious condition had arisen. With these mountain monasteries open to all who came, they had become a refuge for the disaffected. Suppose a man had trouble with his family, he would become religious and retire to a monastery as a monk; if a man failed in business, he might find refuge there; for one reason or another it was easy for a man who was vicious or a failure or unhappy to seek escape in the mountain monasteries. Thousands flocked to them until the government became dis-

turbed and about 1660 the king issued an
edict "that no more men with family ties
should desert them in this way and that
all monks who had families living should
doff their religious garb and come back
to the world and support their families
like honest men."

Notwithstanding neglect, poverty, and
limitations the monasteries showed remarkable recuperative power after the destruction wrought by Hideyoshi's armies. Thus,
Pawpchu-sa was practically destroyed and
the great mass of fine buildings now there
has been constructed since. Some of the
great monasteries farther south also suffered severely; yet the damage has been
fully repaired. (Plate II.)

Nor did scholarship completely disap-
pear in these later years. When Dr. Legge
translated Fa-hien's diary into English, he
had four editions of the work at hand —
two Chinese, one Japanese and one Korean; the latter, which bears the date 1726,
was the most satisfactory and was superior
as a piece of book-making.

KOREAN BUDDHISM:
CONDITION

WITH the exile of Buddhism to the mountains several results ensued. In the first place each monastery became a thing by itself; there was no unity, no combination, no force in the movement of Buddhism as such, over the kingdom. In the second place, not being permitted to enter the cities, the Buddhist priests came to be looked upon with contempt by the people; they were, of course, beggars, vowed to poverty—they had always been that, but they had had respect; with their seclusion in the mountain monasteries they lost what honor had been attributed to them; they became ignorant, vicious and depraved.

In his *History of Korea* Dr. Hulbert says:

" In 1902, a very determined attempt to revive the Buddhist cult was made. The Emperor consented to the establishment of a great central monastery for the whole country in the vicinity of Seoul, and in it a Buddhist high priest who was to control the whole church in the land. It was a ludicrous attempt, because Buddhism in Korea is dead."

Remember at just what point in the history of the nation this effort to restore Buddhism took place. Japan's war against China was declared in 1894; it ended in 1895, with the treaty of Shimonoseki; it was one of the most important wars of recent times; it was fought over Korea — in order to see whether Korea owed allegiance to China or was an independent nation. From 1895 on, Korea was a hotbed of world intrigue. China, Russia, Japan, all were struggling on the peninsula for a continued foothold. Each was trying to gain advantage. From this condition, in 1904 came the great war between Japan and Russia, which was ended by the treaty of Portsmouth. It too, was a war on account of Korea. It decided the question as to whether Russian, or Chinese, or Japanese influence should preponderate.

The year 1902 came right between those two great wars, which were fought on account of Korea. In 1902 the man who had been King—the last real representative of the Yi Dynasty had become Emperor. One of the results of the war of 1894 was to make Korea an empire, and her king an emperor. The effort to reestablish and revive Buddhism was made then during this period of the empire.

The passage quoted from Hulbert was printed in 1905. It referred to an attempt made in 1902, which he says failed, since Buddhism was dead. To-day is 1918. I have been visiting Korea since 1911 and have seen what seems to be definite growth and revival of the old religion. Buddhism appears to-day to be very far from dead in Korea. It shows signs of active life and there may be prospects of its future growth and large development.

The monasteries of Korea are under control of thirty head monasteries.[5] Some of these have only two or three unimportant subordinate monasteries, but others are the heads of really great groups. For

PLATE XII
HAIN-SA: BUILDING FOR THE WOOD-BLOCKS

[Page 27]

instance, Yuchom-sa, in the heart of the
Diamond Mountains, is the head of forty
monasteries in that remarkable mass of
peaks (Plates III, XVII); Pongeum-sa,
which is near Seoul, is said to be the head
of eighty-six monasteries. These head
monasteries in 1902 had become greatly
reduced in property, membership, influence and splendor. They were estranged
from each other. There was no feeling of
unity among them. Each monastery was
a thing by itself and decay and corruption
were everywhere evident.

But about six years ago the priests of these
thirty head monasteries came together;
they held a great meeting and discussed
their common interests; they decided
that union was necessary and a forward
movement, a thing such as was tried
in 1902 and which failed then. It was
tried again and has not failed. They
elected a president of their commission,
with a term of office of one year. His
whole time is devoted to the interests of
united Korean Buddhism for that year.
(Plate I.) They bought property in the

city of Seoul and erected a central building, partly temple and partly office building. The expenses of this head office are borne by the thirty temples in proportion to their importance and wealth. The monasteries are graded into five groups and each contributes annually a set sum for the advancement of Buddhism in the peninsula.

While in Seoul last year, I visited a theological seminary of Buddhism. It has a good location in a desirable part of the city; it occupies a fine old Korean building; it has a corps of teachers of some ability; I found sixty-five students in attendance. The institution had been running for about three years. Most of the students were already connected with some of the mountain monasteries; they had come in for information, for improvement, for further study; they were looking forward to return to their temples with new strength and vigor for their work. The young men with whom I talked seemed to be earnestly interested and anxious for improvement. A definite course of three years instruction is offered to them. The number of students has grown steadily and no doubt the time will come when there will be hundreds of students in this institution.

There is to-day a magazine conducted in the interests of Korean Buddhism. It has been published for something like six years. The history of the editor, Yi Nung Hwa, is rather interesting.[6] His father is a pillar of the Presbyterian Church in Seoul, one of the most successful of the mission churches. The young man himself was educated in Catholic schools in Seoul; his education came from foreigners, and he is now official interpreter for the Belgian Consul; but he finds his pleasure and outside interest in this magazine for the advancement of Korean Buddhism. Son of a Presbyterian Elder, trained in Catholic schools, speaking French, Korean, Chinese and Japanese, professionally engaged in service at a foreign consulate, he is the editor of a magazine for Buddhist propaganda!

Mr. Yi is also the author of a history of

Korean Buddhism, which had not yet been printed when I saw him. It is, I think, the only history that has been written covering the entire field of Korean Buddhism. Everything that is printed in Korea must pass under the eye of the Japanese government, and can be printed only with its permission. It makes no difference whether the material is secular or religious, social, economic, literary or political. At the time when we were speaking about his book it had been sent in to the government for examination. It is to be hoped that it was approved and that permission was given for its publication. A book of that kind would have importance and no such book exists, in any modern form certainly, for popular reading.

One of the most interesting things in connection with this modern movement of Korean Buddhism, and one which seems to show that it has real vitality, is the fact that Buddhist books for common reading are being printed. Most Korean books are printed in Chinese characters and are thus sealed to the common people; they can be

PLATE XIII

HAIN-SA: BUILDING FOR THE WOOD-BLOCKS, INTERIOR

[Page 27]

read only by scholars or people of considerable education. Yet Korea is said to have invented one of the most perfect systems of writing that the world has seen. It is known as the *on-mun* and is competent to write the language perfectly and easily. But scholars in Korea have never used the *on-mun;* it has been considered suitable only for the ignorant, for women and children. If a book is to reach the common people, however, and be widely read, it should be printed in *on-mun*. The books issued by the foreign missionaries in their propaganda have been printed in *on-mun,* or in a mixed script of Chinese character and *on-mun*. The fact that several Buddhist books have recently appeared printed in *on-mun* shows that Korean Buddhism is reaching out after the common people.

Two of these books deserve special mention. One is called the " Eight Scenes from the Life of Buddha." It follows quite closely the story of Buddha's life as told in other countries. The book is widely offered at book stores and street stalls and is said to have considerable sale. More interest-

ing than it, however, is the allegory called
Sei-yeu-ki. You remember that in the
seventh century a Chinese pilgrim, Hiouen
Tsiang, went on foot from China to India,
and that he came back loaded with books
and images for use in religious worship.
That pilgrim was really a historic character, and he wrote an account of his
journey, a simple and charming diary of
travel. His book was called *Sei-yeu-ki,*
which in its English translation appears
under the title of "A Report of Buddhist
Kingdoms." In it he described the countries through which he had passed, the
monasteries and temples which he had seen,
and the adventures he had undergone.
Now in the thirteenth century a Chinese
monk wrote a book with almost the same
name. As pronounced there is scarcely
any difference; when the names are written
they are easily distinguished. The writer intended to imitate the name of the diary of
the old pilgrim. In his story, he says that
a certain man named Hiouen-Tsiang — he
uses the actual name of the old pilgrim —
goes on a journey to the West for books,

idols and information, just as the real
pilgrim did; but instead of telling a true
and simple story this man writes an allegory something of the nature of " Pilgrim's
Progress." It is full of astonishing adventures. It seems that the Emperor of China
died and came to life again. He determined to send Hiouen-Tsiang, "the Master," to the West for books, idols and
pictures. The Master started upon his
errand and as he travelled picked up a
strange group of comrades. The Emperor
had given him a white horse, and of course
he had to have a boy to take care of it; in
addition he had for companions and helpers
a monkey and a pig. The master and his
three human companions were gone, like the
real pilgrim, about fifteen years; they travelled, of course, through the same countries,
but had startling adventures. The master
was very pious, but unpractical; in fact he
was a weak subject for the hero of a story.
But the monkey was fine, and when they got
into trouble it was always the monkey who
rescued them. When the master, through
his lack of knowledge, and practical ex-

perience, was caught by the most palpable traps and tricks only the monkey could rescue him. Yet they all abused the poor creature. All were jealous of him and on the slightest occasion pig or boy or horse urged the master to make the magic hat equipped with thorns and pins squeeze and hurt the monkey's head in order "that he shall not become proud." It is really an interesting and beautiful allegory. It has recently been translated into English by a missionary in China and anyone who wishes may read it. For hundreds of years it has been read in the original Chinese by Chinese, Koreans and Japanese. To-day Koreans may read it in their own language, printed in *on-mun*.

All these signs of life seem to show that Korean Buddhism is far from dead. It is coming forth from its mountain exile and bids fair to make itself felt in the future.

Let us examine for a moment the organization of an ordinary monastery. The monasteries are scattered through the mountains. Many of them are in remote places and it is difficult to reach them. Some are so far back that it would be impossible for them to go farther. I have no fears that ordinary tourists will spoil my delight in Pawp-chu-sa, or Hain-sa, or Yu-chom-sa. If one desires to see them he must pay the price. Take Pawpchu-sa for instance. To see it we dismounted from the railroad train and took a Ford car across country ten miles to a little district capital; the next day, by government automobile, we went out over a road which had just been put in good order — there was only one break in it that was serious; for forty miles we travelled over this mountain road, deeper and deeper among the hills, up and up into the narrowing valley, until with mountains on all sides of us we reached the village of Poun. There we abandoned the automobile. The party went by horses, but a chair had been provided for my benefit. I hate chairs, and would have much preferred a horse, though Korean horses are little creatures and disagreeable. Their gait is as bad as anything one can imagine; there is nothing like a saddle, but only a broad cushion, without stirrups, and the trav-

eller's legs hang down over the front of
the cushion, one foot on each side of the
horse's neck and the rider has no control
whatever over the horse; nor has anyone
else, although the *mapu,* or "boy," runs
along beside and hangs on to the halter or
strikes the beast with stick or whip. I hate
a Korean horse, but I hate a chair worse.
However, we started, the rest on horses.
When we had gone about half a mile the
chair carriers, though professionals, declared they could go no farther; this, of
course, was a mere question of weight; it
was, however, a great relief to me.
Promptly an exchange was made with my
little Japanese photographer and interpreter, who took the chair, while I mounted
his horse — the smallest and weakest of the
outfit. We travelled on and on for miles;
we passed one ridge behind another and
another and another, until at last we
reached Pawpchu-sa. Anyone who really
journeys to Pawpchu-sa has my regard and
blessing.

The trip to Hain-sa, where the wood-
blocks are preserved, is a trying one. We

PLATE XIV
GREAT BUDDHA RELIEF ON ROCK FACE: INNER KONGO
[Page 70]

went by *basha*. Japanese *bashas* are bad; the Japanese themselves think them far superior to Korean, but I prefer the latter. A *basha* is made for six passengers, but usually carries eight. The Japanese *basha* has two benches running lengthwise at the sides; three persons fill a bench, four over-fill one. The driver sits in front and a single horse moves the conveyance. Such is the Japanese *basha*. The Korean vehicle has no benches at the sides like the Japanese affair; the passengers sit upon the floor with thin, rush mats under them, probably to keep the floor of the vehicle clean; there are no springs and the roads are rough. After travelling sitting on the springless floor for thirty-two miles, we abandoned the *basha*, as there was no longer a cart-road, and rode about seventeen miles on horses; it was like travelling over Mexican trails. Thus we reached Hain-sa. I do not begrudge a visit to Hain-sa to any person; those who make the journey deserve to be treated as friends and brothers.

Each monastery has its official corps. First comes the head priest. He has a hard time of it. He has to deal with the outside world and to oversee everything; he is business manager; he has little to do with spiritual direction, but has to settle all the quarrels and deal with all the problems that present themselves to the monastery; he gets all the hard work and shoulders all the blame. He receives, however, some extra rice and is entitled to an extraordinary exhibition of respect. He has a councillor to help him in problems of a serious nature. Next comes the religious head, who leads the services and sees that they are properly observed. The first religious service of the day comes at three o'clock A.M. At that hour the visitor hears the bells and gongs and the droning of songs and prayers. The people of the monastery all turn out to early service. There may be other services throughout the day; there are also times of meditation, and in special halls, where no disturbance is permitted, persons spend hours or entire days in silence and pious thought. There is always a steward whose business it is to attend to the food supply of the entire monastery. In a monastery of a hundred and fifty or two hundred persons in a remote mountain district, the steward's work is important and exacting. At every monastery there are, of course, one or two cooks, whose business it is to prepare the food. There is regularly also, a group of little fellows, boys from ten to fifteen years of age, whose business it is to help these others on every occasion when help is needed. These boys have little in the way of religious duties, but sweeping and cleaning, errands, burden carrying and hard work in general falls on them. (Plate XI.)

The balance of the population in a monastery is devoted to religious living. These include three different kinds of persons — priests, acolytes and orphans. The monasteries have always been orphan asylums. When a child in the country around is left without parents or other proper guardians he is usually sent to the mountain monastery; unless the unexpected happens he will grow up in the way of religion and become a priest or monk when the time arrives.

Many young men come in from the outside world for purposes of instruction. They look forward to becoming monks, but during their period of study they let their hair grow long, dress as outsiders and are regarded as still belonging to the world. Most of them, however, carry out their intention and remain permanently in the monastery. Thirdly, there are the regular monks and priests. They are dressed, of course, in characteristic style, and their heads are shaved. They live on vegetarian food and are vowed to celibacy. At some of the more important monasteries there is a resident teacher, but most of them depend upon a teacher sent from the head temple. The greeting given him when he arrives is beautiful to see. All know when he is expected, and at the hour they go in procession, dressed in their best robes, out to the farthest gate to meet him. When he arrives all but the head priest prostrate themselves so that they actually grovel in the dust. Then, accompanying him, with the head priest walking before, the whole company goes back to the monastery and

PLATE XV

SARI MONUMENT TO MUHAK: HOIAM-SA

[Page 73]

the teaching almost immediately begins. He barely takes a little refreshment and rests a bit before he undertakes his duties. During the period of his stay the teaching continues throughout the day. One class or group comes in after another; the teaching is sometimes from books, sometimes from the teacher's own experience and knowledge.

Are the monasteries really places of great learning; are they centers of deep piety? It is hard to tell and much depends on one's definition.

We must remember that there are two vastly different kinds of Buddhism. They are almost opposite; the one is certainly the negation of the other. The first is the Buddhism which the actual Buddha taught. You remember that he was an historic character, who lived at about five hundred years before Christ. An Indian prince, he is known under various names as Sakyamuni, Siddartha and Gautama. He pondered much over the problems of life and devoted himself to the solution of mysteries; he tried asceticism and listened to one teacher after another; he wandered, medi-

tated, fasted; he finally reached enlightenment. He decided that life was an illusion
and a snare which one would gladly be rid
of; he discovered that the chain that bound
one to this existence could be broken. Release comes from careful conduct; it comes
through right living, and right thinking;
it comes in course of time, after many many
existences; through right living in one life
man gathers *karma* which carries him to
higher and higher stages until at last he
becomes a great scholar; finally he becomes
a Bodhisattva, which is but one step from
Buddha-hood; and finally, from a Bodhisattva, through enlightenment, he becomes a true Buddha and when his earthly
life ends, passes out into oblivion, blissful,
calm nothingness.

Buddha was one of the greatest of world
teachers. His teaching was simple; we
may work out release gradually from the
thraldom into which we are born; through
careful thought and right living we may
pass from stage to stage until at last we
merge into infinity and lose our individu-
ality.

Buddha taught that we end in *Nirvana;*

PLATE XVI

HEAD-PRIEST AND PAGODA: SINKEI-SA, DIAMOND
MOUNTAINS

[Page 74]

his doctrine was a revolt against the idea of an individual soul that lives forever; in his religion there were no figures, no idols, nothing for worship. Buddhism proper taught nothing about gods. It simply taught men to strive for enlightenment, to become Buddhas and to pass out into *Nirvana*.

But this is not the Buddhism of China, Korea or Japan. The Buddhism of these three countries recognizes an individual soul that continues. It has scores of gods and represents them by images or idols; the man who lives to-day does not try to work out salvation for himself through stage after stage of higher living. On the contrary he seeks salvation through another and that other is Amida Buddha. The Koreans call him Amida Pul. You may see them any day standing outside the temples repeating over and over again the formula, "Namu Amida Pul, Namu Amida Pul, Namu Amida Pul." They are thereby gaining salvation; through faith in Amida they will reach the Western Paradise. There was no Western Paradise in

Buddha's teaching; there was no continued existence of the human soul; there was no one through whom men might be saved; one must work out his own salvation. But in this second Buddhism, any person in a single moment may gain salvation. It makes no difference whether a man has led a good or evil life, death-bed repentance may save him. A man does nothing for himself; faith only through the merit of another wins salvation — it sounds like good Presbyterian doctrine.

It is evident that these two forms of Buddhism could not diverge more widely than they do. The early Buddhism taught by Sakyamuni is called *Hinayana* or the "Little Vehicle." The other form is known as *Mahayana* the "Great Vehicle." Korean Buddhism is and for the most part always has been *Mahayana,* yet in the Buddhist temples of the Korean monasteries one finds many a figure of Sakyamuni and the worshippers seem totally unconscious of their inconsistency and of the fact that their worship of Sakya is a contradiction in terms.

PLATE XVII

MAIN TEMPLE: YUCHOM-SA, DIAMOND MOUNTAINS

[Page 35]

This leads us to inquire regarding sects. Japanese Buddhism is divided into many. Thus we may speak of Shingon, Jodo, Zen, or Nichiren Buddhism there. Each of these names stands for a definite system of doctrinal belief. Every student of Buddhism in Japan knows the fundamental differences upon which the dozen or more Japanese Buddhist sects are based. Knowing something of these divisions in Japan it was natural to ask on coming into contact with Korean Buddhism what sects they have. The answer was always immediate and glibly given. "We have two sects — *Syen* and *Kyo*."

This was said everywhere, but I cannot see that there is anything in Korean Buddhism like the sects of Japan. In Shingon there is a whole series of doctrines and beliefs and practices; so in Zen, so in every other sect. Every person belonging to a given sect holds those dogmas and practises those ceremonials characteristic of his sect. No man is at once Shingon and Zen. But in a Korean monastery we find Syen people meditating and Kyo people reading

and to-morrow the situation will be re-
versed, and it seems as if the terms apply
merely to two modes of discipline, not to
actually different sects. At all events in
the same monastery we regularly find Syen
and Kyo.

The texts of Mahayana Buddhism were
originally in Sanskrit. They have been
translated into Chinese and it is in their
Chinese form that they are generally
studied in China, Korea and Japan.[7] In
Korean monasteries we not infrequently
find books that are printed, at least in part,
in Sanskrit characters. Do the Korean
monks know the Sanskrit language? Far
from it. I doubt whether there are a half-
dozen priests in all Korea who know anything whatever of the language.

At every temple one may secure *tarani*.
A *tarani* is a sheet of paper with something
printed on it in red from a wood-block.
The wood-blocks at the different temples
vary and while most of the characters in
the printing are Chinese, there is a sprink-
ling of Sanskrit. A *tarani* is a sort of pass-
port to the Western Paradise and it is

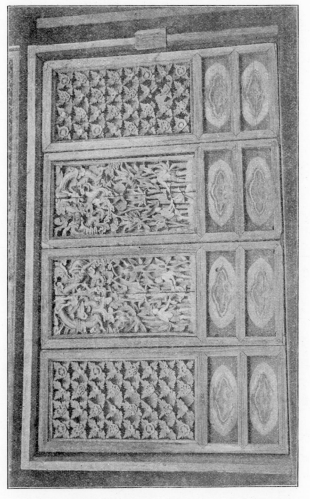

PLATE XVIII
CARVED DOOR: YUCHOM-SA

[Page 82]

supplied for burial with the dead. When a man is burned or buried a *tarani* is placed with his body. We secured them from almost every monastery visited. Perhaps no priest in Korea can read them. We saw, however, at one monastery, an old book concerning *tarani,* and it seems probable that these texts have been copied from such books. About sixty years ago there seems to have been a special fancy for cutting these wood-blocks for printing *tarani* and most of those we saw date from that time.

Interesting are *sari* monuments. As we neared Yuchom-sa we passed ten or twelve stone monuments with a square base, a swelling body and decorated tip. We were told that these were *sari* stones and that in them a *sari* or "jewel" was buried. These *sari* are curious things. It is said that when the body of a monk of special piety is burned a little pebble will be found among the ashes. It is irregular in form, clearly shows fusion, and looks a little like a gem or crystal. It is believed that it has been formed from the elements

[55]

of the dead body, and they say that only about one man out of four hundred gives rise to one of these *sari*.

I had always had my doubts about them. One day at Songkwang-sa, where the monks are exceptionally depraved, a policeman was with us to see that nothing happened. Coming to some *sari* stones we asked a monk about them. He told us the same story that we had heard before and we asked him if he really believed that it was true. He answered, "O yes, surely it is true." The policeman, however, expressed vigorous doubt. The monk replied, "You don't believe it, I will show you." So we proceeded to tear a *sari* monument to pieces! It seemed a shocking thing to do. We took off the top stone, and laid it by, and then turned the main stone upside down. At the center was a little cavity which was neatly covered with a thin sheet or disk of earthenware; removing this we found inside a hole filled with packing, in which was a small tin capsule bearing an inscription. This was said to be the name of the man who had honored the dead

PLATE XIX

BRAHMANIC GUARDIAN OF BUDDHISM: SONGKWANG-SA

[Page 79]

priest by erecting the monument to him. Opening the capsule it was found to contain some packing in the midst of which was the little gem — all that remained to represent the worthy dead man. We put it back with care, replaced the packing, closed the capsule, repacked it and reconstructed the monument as it had been originally. No doubt all these *sari* stones really contain some such relic. That policeman had his doubts — I still have doubts as to just what *sari* are, but it seems certain that all *sari* stones really have *sari* in them.

There is no question that there is much ignorance and even vice among the monks. In this monastery where we examined the matter of *sari* stones there were only five men, poor, ignorant fellows. We early noticed that the head priest there lacked a tooth, but only found after we had left the place that the most devout of the five monks had knocked it out the day before, having had a fight with his superior. The neighbors told us that that monastery was a place of constant disorder and bad conduct.

At one monastery we were even moved
to give a lesson in behavior. Here we were
accompanied by a Japanese policeman; he
was with us to protect and give such aid as
possible, but was absolutely of no use.
The monks received us coldly, answered a
few questions and then disappeared. Un-
accustomed to such treatment, I complained
to the policeman who replied, "This monastery has a very bad name in all this
district; the monks are avaricious; they are
thieves; they always treat visitors badly;
they do nothing unless they are well paid.
That is why I came with you." I replied,
"Why don't you do something, then? Tell
them to come out and do their duty." He
shook his head sadly and said, "You do not
know the reputation of this temple here-
abouts; it has a very bad name indeed."

So turning to my interpreter I said, "We
must deal with this problem right here."
Calling a priest I said to him, "I under-
stand that in this monastery you have a bad
name; there is no time to waste; we want no
delays; call every monk and priest here
at once."

PLATE XX A

DEVA KING, GUARDIAN OF WORLD QUARTER:
SUKWANG-SA

[Page 79]

PLATE XX B
DEVA KING, GUARDIAN OF WORLD QUARTER:
SUKWANG-SA

[Page 79]

He did so, and when they had come I placed them in a semicircle before me and spoke to them. "You are Buddhists; you bear the name of Buddha, a great teacher; he was kind and good and cared nothing for money; he desired to help people and make them better, and people who are Buddhists should be like him; I am told that you are avaricious and when visitors come here you treat them with unkindness and discourtesy unless they pay you well; I shall pay you nothing, but I want you to think of the disgrace you bring upon your name by such conduct; I am visiting the monasteries because I wish to see whether Buddhism is a living force in this land; I wish to see how you monks live and what your conduct is, and what the people say about you; go back to your rooms and think over what I have said; as I go from place to place, looking at things here, I expect to have them open, and I wish you to treat me as a brother and a friend; remember that others who may come after me deserve equally good treatment; it is a shame to bring disgrace upon a cause."

Well, there was an instant conversion. Poor, ignorant fellows, living in their remote mountain monastery, how should they know better? They gave me honey water and popped rice; they showed me their buildings and their treasure; they begged that I would come again and some accompanied me, when I was leaving, down to the outer gate.

As for ignorance, it is probable that very few of them could pass examination on any kind of Buddhism, whether Hinayana or Mahayana. What more could be expected? Surely we can scarcely throw stones. What do most of us know about Christian doctrine? How wise religiously are the common people in our churches? In a recent newspaper it was stated that a man among us asked five professional men about the Holy Ghost. Do you suppose he got much in the way of a satisfactory answer? In reality he got nothing. All these educated men had other business than to know about the Holy Ghost. They were not well informed in regard to the religion in which they had been reared; and yet we

PLATE XXI

GIGANTIC DEVA KING, GUARDIAN OF WORLD
QUARTER: PAWPCHU-SA

(The Korean standing by is a man of normal stature)

[Page 80]

expect Buddhists, who have been exiled in mountain monasteries for four hundred years to know so much!

How is the population of the monasteries maintained? Whence do new members come to-day? There is, of course, always a supply of orphan children, few of whom ever go back into the world after they have been brought up in monastery surroundings. Other people drift in for many reasons. Men who have lost their friends and relatives by death often go to the monasteries. So do those who fail in business, or who have been disappointed in life enterprises. The head-priest of one small, but very famous, ancient monastery, only recently became religious; he had been employed as a janitor or helper in a Buddhist temple of Japanese in a Korean city and became interested and attracted. The head-priest of one of my favorite monasteries was in the world until he had reached the age of fifty years or more; he had been in military service and I believe, had risen to the rank of Colonel; getting on in years, however, he began to think

seriously of religious matters and retreated
to the monastery. With one young priest
at Yuchom-sa in the Diamond Mountains
we talked for hours, until midnight. He
was genuine; he had the spirit of true religion; he was a thinker and was in the
monastery from principle. There are no
doubt many like him.

We were at Tongdo-sa on Buddha's
birthday. It is one of the great monasteries
of the South. They knew we were coming
and therefore we found a place to sleep.
When we were within three or four miles
of it we found ourselves in a crowd of
persons going up to the celebration. The
nearest railway station is about ten miles
away. Most of the people, however, had
walked from their homes. It is a mountain
district, sparsely settled; there are surely
only two or three towns of any size within
fifteen miles of the place. When we
reached the monastery we found one of the
liveliest scenes we ever witnessed in Korea.
The head-priest told us that ten thousand
people slept on the grounds of the temple
that night. The majority of them were

women. Of course, *that* would have been true if it had been a Presbyterian gathering. We were two nights there. On the full day that we spent with them a wonderful crowd of people was present; there were a few Japanese — a teacher and one or two officials — but apart from these the multitude was Korean. Probably fifteen thousand people were there that day. We found that one of the events of that evening was a moving-picture show in one of the monastery buildings. The life of Buddha was to be represented in moving pictures. All this does not look much like death! It is said that at the other head monasteries there were proportionately equal crowds.

We often asked what efforts were being made at monasteries for general improvement and helping the outside world. The purpose of a monastery, of course, is not related to such undertakings. In all religions, at all times, monasteries have been only for persons who were seeking individual improvement or salvation. In their very essence they are not philanthropic or reform movements. Still, with the lack of temples in the cities and definite teaching of the people through them, it might seem as if something would be undertaken by the monasteries. In reality there is much more in this direction than could be expected. At several of the monasteries there is a school for outside children; some have undertaken a definite work of teaching and some others realize that they have a genuine opportunity to aid in the elevation of the country. More and more the monasteries seem to awake to the existence of these possibilities.

Korean Buddhism has, perhaps, a political part to play. When the Japanese took over Korea, Buddhists came into the country in great numbers. Japanese priests and temples came with these settlers. These priests and temples are in the cities and larger towns. They do not, however, fit with the Koreans. There might be thousands of them and they would still not make Korean converts — not because the Japanese are not ready to do mission work, but because the Koreans are not ready to accept it. The Korean Buddhism of to-day is actually Korean, not Japanese.

I can imagine nothing that would be more dangerous to Japanese control than a strong and vital Korean Buddhism that was hostile to Japan. On the other hand, I can think of nothing that would be a greater help to Japan than a Korean Buddhism developed among those people by their own priests and friendly to Japan. What Korean Buddhism is to be in the future depends upon its relation to the government now there. If Korean Buddhism accepts and coöperates with the Japanese control, it will become the mightiest factor that can be devised to make Japan's hold on the peninsula secure. If hostile to Japan, when the crisis comes, as it surely will come, when Japan will be tried out again and once for all on Korean soil, Korean Buddhism may be the decisive element in that moment of test.

KOREAN BUDDHISM: ART

TO-NIGHT we are to consider art in Korean Buddhism. We shall examine it under six different forms — scenery, sculpture in stone, wood carving, architecture, images or idols and painting.

Perhaps it scarcely seems to you as if scenery — real landscape, not landscape painting — were art. In the Orient, however, it is surely such. Eastern peoples have for hundreds of years been passionately fond of the beautiful in nature. Chinese, Koreans, Japanese will travel on foot or by any possible conveyance many miles to see a famous view. They locate their houses in pretty places; they build temples and shrines upon commanding points. When the Korean monks, in the fifteenth century, were compelled to take refuge in the mountains, they located their buildings in surroundings harmonious to

PLATE XXII

WALL PAINTING: THE WHITE TORTOISE SCENE OF THE *Sei-yeu-ki*: PONGEUM-SA

[Page 83]

the religion. Their locations have been chosen with great care. And there is much more in scenery than the careless spectator thinks; for the Oriental scenery always contains something of the esoteric.

For example, think of the Diamond Mountains. They are a remarkable tangle of peaks and ridges; measuring only thirty or forty miles across, the area is more or less elliptical in form; it is called "the twelve thousand peaks" or summits. The Diamond Mountains have been famous for two thousand years, and famous not only in Korea, but in China and Japan. They have been the theme of hundreds of poems and have furnished material for scores of books, some of them hundreds of years old. Artists have delighted in depicting their beauties. The Diamond Mountains with their twelve thousand peaks are divided into two portions. The name Diamond Mountains in itself is most suggestive; the diamond is one of the most precious symbols in Buddhism — indicating purity, clearness, brightness — and Korean Buddhism was a religion of light and illumination. The two divisions of the Diamond Mountains are known as the Inner and the Outer Kongo. The traveller may visit the outer region and realize but little of the true significance of Kongo-San. In the Inner Kongo every outstanding rock is significant. Every building has been placed with reference to some hidden meaning of the landscape, and with every step the visitor goes deeper and deeper into mystery.

Let us approach a mountain monastery. The trail is well marked long before we see the buildings. Once upon the grounds we come to some of those carved posts or pillars, devil posts, *changson,* which were illustrated in the preceding lecture, and were no doubt taken over from the old-time paganism. We pass through the outer gate. All the gates bear names significant to the thoughtful worshipper. We pass through gate after gate like " the gateway of Life," " the gate of All-powerful Truth," " the gate of Illumination." Many of these gates are pavilions, resting-places, whence one may view the scenery, or visit with

PLATE XXIII

Wall Paintings on Plaster: Sukwang-sa

[Page 85]

companions, or meditate in preparation for worship. As we approach the buildings we may find ourselves in a narrowing valley, or passing some cascade. All the rock cliffs have been seized and utilized and bear inscriptions, beautifully cut into the stone material. We see the formula, constantly on the tongue of Korean Buddhists, *Namu Amida Pul*, not once or dozens of times, but everywhere, repeated hundreds of times over. The *Daimon*, or great gateway, is the last; it signifies the gate of death through which we reach the heavenly life.

At last we come to the mass of monastery buildings. Every temple has its name marked clearly on it, sometimes the names themselves are suggestive, helping the worshipper to clearer thought and serious meditation.

The second form of art is sculpture in stone. We have already mentioned the formulæ and other inscriptions cut upon the cliffs. To the Oriental eye they are as beautiful and represent as much artistic skill as figures would. There are, however, also on the natural rock faces,

designs and figures cut in low relief, which
we find in the most unexpected places. In
the Inner Kongo there are many great representations of the Buddhas cut upon the
vertical rock face. Here, for instance, are
three figures, twenty feet in height, one of
the great Buddhist trinities. Again, there
is a representation of Monju, of even
greater size. (Plate XIV.) On another
face of rocks are the figures of the famous
fifty-three Buddhas who came so long ago
to live and die among the Diamond Mountains.

In a former lecture we referred to the
cave chapel of Sukkul-am. It is full of
beauty. Excavated in the slope near a
great ridge summit, it looks out upon the
Eastern Sea. In the old days it was ap-
proached by a fine flight of steps. From
its summit a passageway led to the sub-
terranean chamber. It was bordered on
both sides by slabs carved with figures in
high relief. Here are the two guardian de-
mons, the four kings of the cardinal points,
the six generals. Passing between them we
reach the little circular chapel, about thirty

PLATE XXIV

GREAT FIGURES OF BUDDHIST TRINITY, SEATED: PAWPCHU-SA.
SAKYA, MONJU, FUGEN

[Page 88]

ART

feet across, subterraneously situated in the
hillside. Its low, vaulted roof is an in-
genious and wonderful construction. The
surrounding walls are filled with slabs
bearing fine carvings. Here are three
splendid figures of Bodhisattvas, with
boat-shaped haloes, three other figures of
Bodhisattvas with round haloes, and distrib-
uted between them the ten first disciples
of the Great Teacher. These ten figures
present marvellous detail of feature; not
only personal differences, but race differences are sharply brought out; more than
that the figures were originally colored, and
no doubt, different races are indicated by
the different tints. There is no question
that individuals of different races were
among the first disciples of the Buddha.
And in the center of all this beauty, this
flowering of ancient art, sits the stone
Buddha, on his lotus pedestal. It is a
monolith, cut from a block of stone about
eleven feet in height. It is beautiful in
pose, in feature, and in expression. For
almost fifteen hundred years it has sat there
calmly looking out upon the Eastern Sea.

Every morning it is greeted by the rising sun.

Besides figures cut in high relief, the old artists made full sculptures in the round. Such, of course, was the Buddha figure, just described. Such are the great miriok, sculptured from natural rock pinnacles, like the one at Eunjin. You may remember the picture of a giant lotus pedestal, lying in the courtyard of Kumsan-sa (Plates V, VI), which we showed you in the first lecture; it is at least a thousand years of age. In the same courtyard, you remember that we saw a little tower or pagoda of stone, thirteen stories high, but in reality no taller than a man. At Pawpchu-sa there is that splendid bowl of stone, more than twelve hundred years of age, which in its time, no doubt, was filled with pure water for the cleansing of the hands and mouth of worshippers. Sometimes we find stone lanterns and occasionally these are supported by animal figures in caryatid forms. Then there are the *sari* stones and altars and turtle-borne monuments.

Look at this series of pictures from

PLATE XXV

GREAT FIGURES OF BUDDHIST TRINITY, STANDING:
KUMSAN-SA. AMIDA, KWANNON, DAISEISHI

(Thirty feet or so in height)

[Page 89]

Hoiam-sa, one of the first temples we visited in 1917. (Plate XV.) To-day it is a place of no significance, but it was once a great religious center and has been associated with three famous men. It chanced the day we visited it that the three monks who live there were about to celebrate the day sacred to the memory of these noted teachers; gifts and offerings and all the paraphernalia for worship were laid out, ready. These three men were Muhak, Chikong and Nanong. Chikong was a native of India, who spent his last days in Korea. Nanong was chaplain and preceptor of King Kong-Min-Oang, the last king of the Koryu dynasty. Muhak was the chaplain and preceptor of Yi-tajo, founder of the Yi Dynasty. Behind the monastery building there rises a remarkable narrow-backed and sloping ridge. It bears a line of monuments reared to the memory of these three men. The stones commemorating Chikong and Nanong were erected by Muhak in the year 1393; the stones in memory of him were reared in 1401. The monument to each of these worthies consists of four stone objects — a lantern, an altar, a *sari* stone — which I suppose contains the jewel that was left after the burning of the man in whose honor it was reared — and a stone turtle figure from whose back rises a slab bearing a long inscription. These turtle-stones with inscribed slabs are found everywhere in Korea; the turtle is the symbol of longevity and its use in this connection breathes the wish that the memory of the thing recorded may endure ten thousand years. These monuments are typical and good examples of their class. The carving on Muhak's *sari* stone is particularly beautiful.

In connection with stone work we must remind you again of the towers or pagodas of which you have seen repeated illustrations. Here we show but one to refresh your memory. (Plate XVI.) Such towers or pagodas rise in stories, numbering from three to thirteen, but always odd — three, five, seven, thirteen. There are hundreds of them scattered over the peninsula and at all the old monasteries you will find them.

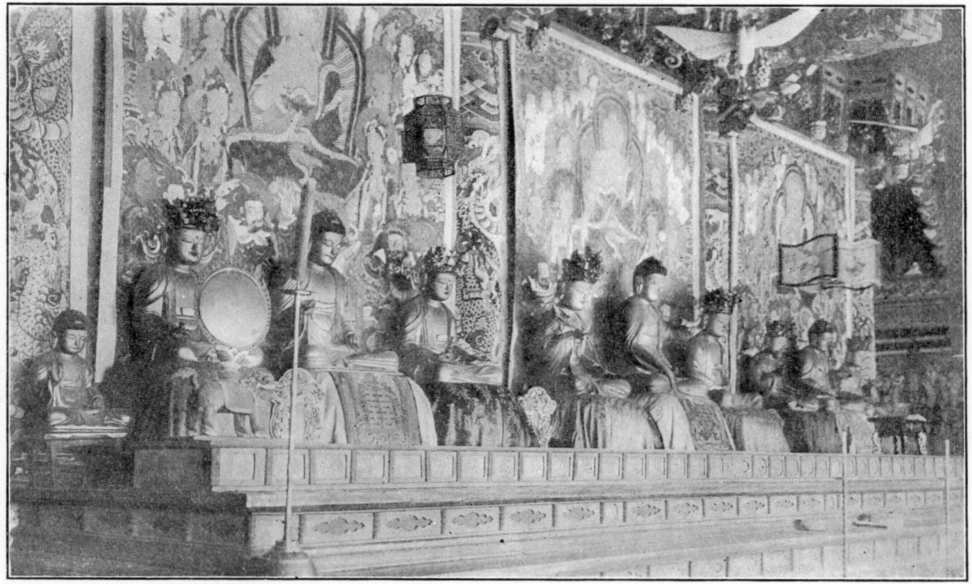

PLATE XXVI

FIGURES — A TRIO OF TRINITIES: SUKWANG-SA

(The figures are said to be Kwannon, Amida, Daiseishi, Monju, Vairoshana, Fugen, Jihi, Sakyamuni, Teikakara)

Some of those in the monasteries of the Diamond Mountains claim to be fifteen hundred years of age or more. They are symbolical, variously; they may denote the life of the individual, pointing heavenward, developing from one stage of perfection to another; they may mean the body of the faithful, or the church; the simple three-story towers symbolize earth, sky and heaven.

Thirdly, are the wooden figures and other carvings in wood. And before we study these in detail let us remember that all religions are accustomed to borrow from those that have preceded them. In Christianity we have quantities of superstition lingering on from our days of paganism. Every religion that attempts a propaganda is compelled to take over much from the faiths which it displaces. India is a veritable mother of religions. One after another great religious systems have developed there. In very ancient days there was the simple nature worship of the old Aryans, as shown us in their sacred hymns, the Vedas. Among their gods two

[75]

of the greatest were Brahma and Indra.
Brahma was the creator, Indra was a
god of heaven, an atmospheric deity who
wielded thunderbolts, who hurled light-
ning strokes against the foe. In course of
time the old Aryans advanced in culture,
and their ancient worship gave way to a
systematized religion, Brahmanism, with
many gods, having definite names and
qualities and attributes. But old Brahma
and Indra lived on from the early days into
Brahmanism. In that system Brahma was
the king of all the gods, Indra was the king
of heaven — having a special heaven of
great beauty. It is said that his heaven was
situated between the four peaks of Meru
and consisted of thirty-two cities of Devas,
eight on each of the four corners of the
mountain. Indra's capital was at the center
where he sat enthroned, with a thousand
eyes and four arms grasping the thunder-
bolt, in company with his wife and eleven
thousand and nine hundred concubines.
There he received monthly reports regarding the progress of good and evil in the
world from his four Maharajas, heavenly

PLATE XXVII
FIGURE AND PAINTING OF KWANNON: POMO-SA
[Page 89]

kings of the cardinal points. The word Deva in Brahmanism is applied to the gods in general; if a god is not specifically named he is called a Deva.

Brahmanism was the religion of India when Buddha came. He devoted his life to its overthrow, and his teaching was hostile to its assumptions. Curiously, however, in the popular traditional life of Buddha many incidents are mentioned in which the friendliest of relations were established between Buddha and the Devas of the old faith. Thus it is said that Brahma himself appeared to Buddha and begged him to begin his teaching. Indra in these stories repeatedly shows his friendship. There is one splendid occasion mentioned in which Buddha had been to Indra's heaven; when he was ready to descend, stairs appeared for him made of the choicest and most beautiful materials, and as he came down this stairway, Brahma descended by a side stairway of silver and Indra upon a stairway of purple gold upon the other side, while with them came thousands of Devas, singing Buddha's praises.

The four Maharajas, heavenly kings of
the cardinal points, who reported to Indra
every month, showed themselves equally
friendly. On one occasion Buddha was
without a begging bowl; the Deva kings
came to him and each one offered a begging-
bowl of emerald; the Buddha refused to
take them, as they were of too precious
material; so they offered bowls less fine and
each was strenuous that he should accept
his gift; so Buddha took the four bowls
and placing them together, lo, they became
a single bowl, but with a rim showing how
four had merged, so that none of the kind
Devas was neglected or hurt in feeling, and
the offering of all was accepted by the Great
Teacher; it is said that this begging bowl
was in existence hundreds of years after
Buddha's time, kept as a precious treasure
in a temple.

We need not then, be surprised, to find
that a number of the old Brahmanic gods
were taken bodily over into Buddhism.
Brahma and Indra are in fact to-day considered in Mahayana to be the chief
patrons and protectors of Buddhism. The

PLATE XXVIII

HALL OF THE TEN KINGS OF HELL: YONGJU-SA

(Notice combination of figures and painting; the god of hell with two helpers, five kings with small
servants, two other officers, and one of the two Brahmanic guardians)

[Page 91]

four Maharajas have also been taken over completely. And Yama, the very ancient god of hell, to-day finds himself as comfortable in Buddhism as he ever could have been in Brahmanism, or in the earlier Aryan worship of the Vedas.

Approaching any Buddhist temple in Japan or Korea you are almost sure to find two gigantic figures standing at the outer gate. They are the old gods Brahma and Indra. They are represented as full-muscled men of gigantic size, wrestling against the powers of evil. (Plate XIX.)

At another gate, farther up the trail, one is almost sure to find the Maharajas, heavenly kings of the cardinal points, under shelter, each in a niche or alcove; usually there are two on either side as one passes through the gate.[8] Being related to the cardinal points, they are always arranged in the same order, and are distinguished from each other by having different colored faces, each having the color proper to the district over which he has control. (Plate XX, a, b.) Each carries a characteristic object, thus one bears a pagoda or tower on his hand, another carries a blazing jewel, the third varies what he carries, but frequently he plays upon a lute, the fourth one has a sword; these four great Brahman deities are found to-day in Korea at every Buddhist monastery, at the gate commonly called "the gate of the four kings"; there they watch, guarding the monastery against all harm. These are almost always figures of wood, but rarely one may find paintings on the wooden walls instead of the figures. While these guardian kings are always represented in heroic size the series at Pawpchu-sa are of extraordinary dimensions, probably the largest in Korea. (Plate XXI.)

Yama, too, was taken over from the older faith. The god of hell, he was assisted by ten helpers; each of these served as his representative in a separate hell, or division of that place of torment. Yama judges souls and inflicts penalties, assigns duties, and directs all the details of his realm. In most Korean monasteries there will be a hall of the ten kings in which we see figures of Yama with his assistants.

PLATE XXIX

HALL OF FIVE HUNDRED RAKAN: SUKWANG-SA

[Page 90]

Next we may consider architecture. We place it fourth because we have pursued a logical order of approach. Coming through the beautiful scenery, we have passed over the trail, noticing the inscriptions on the cliffs, passing by the guardians of the outer gate, walking between the four kings on their ceaseless guard, but at last have come to the monastery buildings proper and see them in their age and beauty before us. We have already seen representations of many of these temples in the preceding lectures. You have noticed that all were built of wood; you have observed the curious mode of timbering; you have studied the tangle of projecting timber ends under the roof — the decorative features applied to them, the carving and painting; red, green, black, white and blue, the gaudiest of colors are used upon them in a fashion which we could not conceive, and from which we would expect disharmony, though the real effect is charming. You have examined in detail the carved decoration of the doors, sometimes foliage, again floral, or with figures mingled with the other designs. (Plate XVIII.)

While the buildings themselves are always of wood there is a curious use made of stone at times in the way of supports. You remember in a picture from Sukwang-sa this was illustrated. The building was in the nature of a pavilion where tablets bearing names were left by visitors; the pavilion was borne upon upright columns of stone, highly characteristic of Korea, but not common elsewhere.

Another feature of the architecture is wall-painting and here we find two different kinds. Pictures may be painted directly upon the woodwork of the wall. It is more common, however, to panel the timbered walls with plastering and then to paint upon the plaster. Let us examine examples of both kinds.

You remember that among the Buddhist books recently printed in *on-mun* was an allegory by a Chinese monk. The writer's name was Chiu-Chang-Chun; he was born in 1208 and died in 1288. His book was named *Sei-yeu-ki;* at Pongeum-sa, a scene

PLATE XXX

EXTRAORDINARY COMBINATIONS OF RAKAN FIGURES: HALL OF FIVE HUNDRED
RAKAN: SONGKWANG-SA

[Page 90]

taken from his book is painted on the wooden wall. We present it as an example of this kind of decoration. It represents a scene from the closing part of the old story. (Plate XXII.)

The pilgrims had almost finished their journey and were returning in state, on cherubim, with a great collection of idols and sacred texts. It was found, however, that they had suffered only eighty trials, and it seems that to be perfect they should pass through eighty-one — nine times nine — so angels were sent to overtake the eight cherubim, and tell them privately that they must let the monks suffer one trial more. This the angels did. As a sample of the story, and in explanation of the picture we quote from Dr. Richard's translation.

"It was a strange sensation to be on the ground again. They had come down near some water. The master asked, 'Can anyone tell me where we are?'

The monkey said, 'Master, this is the mouth of the Milky Way River.' The river was wide. It was also a lonely place, without houses or boats, and they were on the western side. How could they get across? Two of them suggested

that since the master had left his mortal body
behind they could cross the river by magic,
but the monkey said, ' No, it cannot be done.'
He knew that there was one trial more to
undergo, and it was for this they had stopped
on the way. Then they heard a cry, ' Chinese
priest, come this way.' They went and found
that it was the white tortoise, who had ferried
them over as they went West, at the time when
they had saved the family at Chen Kia Chwang.
The tortoise said he had been waiting for their
return for a long time and was glad to see them.
The practical monkey said, ' Formerly we had
to trouble you. Now we meet again.'

At this the four pilgrims were very rejoiced
to see the tortoise. He took them and the
horse all on his back and swam across to the
other side. As they neared the Eastern shore
and it was getting dark, the tortoise said,
' Master, when you went West I asked you to
inquire of Buddha for me how I might return
to my former state, and when I might get a
human body. Did you remember to ask?'
But the master had been so absorbed in his own
affairs that he had completely forgotten the
tortoise and his request and so he had nothing
to say. The tortoise, finding that he had been
forgotten, turned a somersault, and threw all
and everything into the river. Happily the
mortal body of the master had been exchanged

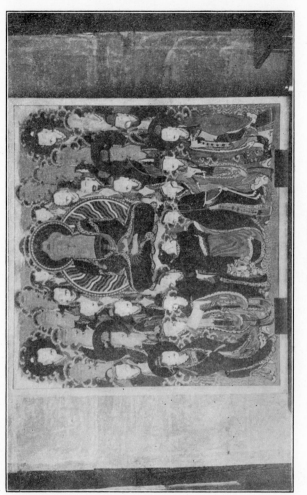

PLATE XXXI
PAINTING OF THE SEVEN STARS: SUKWANG-SA

for an immortal one, and therefore he was safe in the water. The pig and the monkey, the boy and the horse, were also at home in the water, but the books were all soaked."

The old allegory took a strong hold upon Eastern Asia and there must have been hundreds of pictures painted in the course of time representing its incidents.

As an example of the wall-paintings on plaster we may study a group of paintings, each representing an individual being, from one of the main temples at Sukwang-sa. None of these figures is haphazard, or without significance. Each would be recognized by the well-informed Buddhist. (Plate XXIII.)

Fifth are the idols or images. In the Buddhism taught by Sakya there was no room for them. The Great Teacher recognized no gods, and his followers should have no representations of deities. In Amida Buddhism, however, there are many gods, and a multitude of figures. The Buddhas, themselves are all represented among them including Sakya. When we examine the figures worshipped in Buddhist temples we find three groups. (a) Buddhas, (b) Bodhisattvas, (c) Arhats or Rakan. Sakya was not the first Buddha; in fact he was the twenty-fourth or twenty-fifth in the line of those who attained enlightenment and gained *Nirvana*. The Indians reckoned time in long periods or *kalpas;* most of the Buddhas were in former *kalpas,* but even in the present *kalpa,* in which we live, Buddha had three predecessors; and before our *kalpa* ends a successor will appear, Maitreya, or Miroku, the coming Buddha.[9]

The two Buddhas most commonly represented by figures in Korean Buddhism are Sakya and Amida. Miroku, too, is frequently to be seen, but Miroku is not yet a Buddha but only Bodhisattva.

Bodhisattvas were human beings who had piled up *karma* and passed from stage to stage until they stood within a single step of Buddha-hood; during their next existence they could hope for illumination, enlightenment, *Nirvana*. There are many Bodhisattvas, but the ones most commonly represented by Korean figures are six in

PLATE XXXII
GROUP PAINTING: SUKWANG-SA

[Page 95]

number. Their Korean names are Miryek Posal, Titsang Posal, Kwandyeieun Posal, Taiseichi Posal, Mounsou Posal, and Pohien Posal. These Bodhisattvas are much better known to the outside world by their Japanese names, and having introduced them in Korean terminology we shall refer to them as we have opportunity under the Japanese forms.

They become, then, Maitreya or Miroku, Jizo, Kwannon, Daiseishi, Monju, Fugen. Curiously enough in Korean iconography Jizo, a most mild and gentle god, fond of and loved by children, replaces Yama often as the king of hell. Kwannon, god of mercy, usually considered female in Japan, though not invariably, is usually male in Korean representation.

The third type of images of figures worshipped in Korean monasteries are the Arhats or Rakan. These are men who have made progress; they have meditated, studied, listened and thought; some of them are the original students of Sakya; all have gained a store of helpful *karma,* and many of them are worshipped. When made in figures there are two groups of Rakan. One known as the sixteen Rakan, the other as the five hundred. The sixteen Rakan are all absolutely historical personages of early date, friends, relatives, and hearers, of Sakya. In figures and in paintings they are represented with characteristic attributes, readily recognized.

These three kinds of figures are usually made of wood, painted and gilded; sometimes the gold leaf on them represents absolutely considerable value. The figures of the Buddhas and Bodhisattvas are frequently of large size, and often beautiful. They may be standing or seated, but in both cases the position of the hands and fingers is important and significant. (Plate XXIV.) Buddhism everywhere recognizes a series of finger symbols carrying a message. It is interesting to notice that the Buddha is usually included in a trinity. This fact is among many which have led some writers like Professor Lloyd, Doctor Richard, and Madame Gordon to think that Mahayana Buddhism is actually Christianity worked over and given the name of Buddhism.

PLATE XXXIII
ONE OF THE EIGHT SCENES IN THE LIFE OF BUDDHA:
SAKYA GAINS ENLIGHTENMENT: POMO-SA

[Page 91]

Trinities are conspicuous everywhere.
Often we find the central figure of the
three to be Sakya, while to his right and
left are the Bodhisattvas Monju and Fugen.
The former sometimes sits upon a dog or
lion, and the latter upon a white elephant.
Then they are easily recognized by their
mount. When not mounted they are not so
easy of recognition. Even more common
in Korea is the Amida trinity. Amida is
usually accompanied by Kwannon on one
side and Daiseishi on the other. (Plate
XXV.) There are other trinities to be
seen in Korean temples but these two are
common. (Plate XXVI.)

These figures are generally in curious
relation with paintings. In most temples
where there are figures on the altar there
are paintings hung up on the wall behind
which usually represent the same beings as
the figures, but accompanied by many more
attendants. This association of pictures
and figures representing the same being is
rare, if it occurs, in Japanese Buddhism.
(Plate XXVII.)

Lastly, we come to paintings. While

many are related to figures as just mentioned, many more stand by themselves and
are displayed upon the walls of halls and
temples without figures. If we desire to
make a study of the paintings of a monastery we must pass from hall to hall.
Many monasteries are absolute masses of
great buildings. In the main temple there
are usually figures of a trinity of Buddhas
or sometimes even three trinities with paintings hung behind. In the Rakan hall we
may find the sixteen Rakan in figures, in
paintings, or in combinations. In halls of
the five hundred Rakan, we usually find
five hundred little figures set on shelves
thickly around all three sides; no two are
just alike, and it is probable that you will
be told with glee that if you look long enough
you will find your own father represented
among them. (Plates XXIX, XXX.) In
the hall of the Ten Kings of Hell we sometimes find the figures of Yama or of Jizo
with the ten helpers; if so, behind the figures are frightful paintings of the ten hells,
a picture of each one behind its proper king.
Sometimes, however, there are only paint-

PLATE XXXIV
THE GOD OF THE MOUNTAIN: FUKO-AN, BRANCH
OF SINKEI-SA, DIAMOND MOUNTAINS

[Page 93]

ings in this hall. (Plate XXVIII.) At some
temples there is the hall of the Eight Scenes
of the Life of Buddha.[10] These scenes are
definite and fixed in every detail, are traditional, and have been passed down for
centuries. The whole building is occupied
by the eight great paintings hung upon the
wall. Each contains a mass of detail, and
there may be hundreds of individuals represented in a single scene. (Plate XXXIII.)
Occasionally there is a hall of portraits at
a monastery; such a one we saw at the monastery where we rebuked the priests for
avarice and impoliteness; the building is
devoted to the portraits which are said to
be reliable representations of the head
priests of this monastery for a period of
almost fifteen hundred years. One might,
however, visit many monasteries without
finding such a hall.

Probably every monastery of any con-
sequence has its hall of Seven Stars. It is
always a little building and on the out-
skirts of the group of temples. Korea must
have worshipped the constellation of the
Great Bear, the Big Dipper or the Seven

Stars, long before Buddhism came. Many Koreans still pay worship to the stars themselves. The father of a young man who was once my Korean interpreter, never fails to pray to the seven stars on any night when the sky is clear enough for them to be seen; the worship is interesting and deserves attention. It was probably taken over early by Buddhism. The picture always shown in this little hall is very curious. There is always a Buddha figure of some kind in it, but above are Buddha-like figures of the Seven Stars, heavenly beings, with pale faces; below there are the representations of seven earthly ministers corresponding to them; the idea that heavenly conditions are reproduced upon the earth is one common to many religions. (Plate XXXI.)

One other building is certain to be found at every monastery. It is a wee structure, sacred to the God of the Mountain. He is a mysterious being. He is usually represented with a beard and a beard quite different from those regularly seen in China, Korea or Japan. He is always accompanied by a tiger, particularly notice-

PLATE XXXV
PORTRAIT OF ONE OF THE CHIEFS OF THE SIXTEEN
RAKAN: CHIKCHI-SA

[Page 95]

able for head and tail; the god of the mountain varies more than any other representation in Korean art. The features mentioned, however, are always emphasized. All agree that the god of the mountain is individual; he is not the god of mountains generally, nor a god overseeing mountains everywhere, but ever specifically the god of *the* mountain on which his shrine is located. (Plate XXXIV.)

Sometimes there is another very little hall known as the hall of the Lonely Saint. When it occurs it usually stands at the side of the hall of the god of the mountain and is of its size. Within there is a hanging picture of the Lonely Saint. Unfortunately we cannot show a copy of it. We have planned repeatedly to take it but something has always happened to prevent. Trollope tells us that the lonely saint was a historic personage, Chikai, who lived in China in the sixth century, and was the founder of the very ancient Tendai sect.

These paintings in Korean temples are rarely beautiful, but they surely deserve careful study by competent art students.

The colors used are bright and light. Faces of Buddhas and Bodhisattvas are usually yellow or white. These high beings are regularly represented with aureoles, the boat-shaped aureole occurring commonly with Kwannon and Miroku. Gods and human beings occur in crowds in these paintings, but no matter how crowded the composition the individuals are usually definite and known. The artists are priests and it is common for the few who have famous skill to travel from temple to temple, touching up old pictures and painting new ones. They stay for weeks or months and then pass on to new fields. The designs are certainly traditional and very old, but the paintings themselves, as we see them in the temple, are many of them the work of very recent years. Most of the monks and acolytes know very little of the meaning of the pictures, but those who paint them, and those who are serious students can identify the actors in the scenes depicted. We reproduce a picture from Sukwang-sa which illustrates the crowding of persons and the attention given to detail. Upon it

PLATE XXXVI
GREAT PAINTING, PAWPCHU-SA

[Page 96]

PLATE XXXVII

GREAT PAINTING DISPLAYED AT BUDDHA'S BIRTHDAY CEREMONY: TONGDO-SA

[Page 96]

there are represented one Pul or Buddha, with three faces, four Posal or Bodhisattvas, the twenty-eight heavenly kings (each corresponding to one of the ancient constellations), and ten times ten gods (they are actually grouped by tens and there are ten each of earth, fire, water, small water bodies, air, the human body, movement, field work and mountain fortresses). This design is really a common one, and we have a photograph of it also from Pawpchu-sa. Comparison of the two pictures shows absolute identity in the number and placing of the individuals. (Plate XXXII.)

We have already stated that there is considerable variation in the picture of the god of the mountain, though he is always recognizable by certain features. Pictures of individual Rakan are common in temples and these pictures are always precise and definite, giving in every instance the characteristic features or attributes. (Plate XXXV.)

Occasionally—perhaps more commonly than we know—the monasteries possess an enormous rolled painting of a single Buddha. We have seen one at Pawpchu-sa and another at Tongdo-sa. At Pawpchu-sa they brought it out from the great temple and unrolled it for us, in the open, that we might see its size. At Tongdo-sa it was already elevated for the occasion of the celebration of Buddha's birthday. It towered above the highest building, and was worshipped by the crowding thousands. (Plates XXXVI, XXXVII.)

In this brief study of Korean Buddhism we have but sketched a subject which presents a vast material, which as yet is almost unknown and practically untouched by students.

BIBLIOGRAPHY

Gale. *The Pagoda of Seoul*. Transactions of the Korea Branch of the Royal Asiatic Society. Vol. VI, Pt. II, pp. 1–22. Seoul: 1915.

Gordon. *Some Recent Discoveries in Korean Temples and their Relationship to Early Eastern Christianity*. Trans. K. B. R. A. S. Vol. V, Pt. II, pp. 1–39. Seoul: 1914.

Gordon. *Symbols of "the Way"—Far East and West*. Tokyo: 1916. Maruzen & Co.

Hulbert. *History of Korea*. Seoul: 1905. 2 vols. Methodist Publishing House.

Jones. *Colossal Buddha at Eunjin*. Trans. K. B. R. A. S. Vol. I, pp. 51–70. Seoul: 1901.

Richard. *A Mission to Heaven . . . by Ch'iu Ch'ang Ch'un*. Shanghai: 1913. The Christian Literature Society's Depot.

Trollope. *Introduction to the Study of Buddhism in Corea*. Trans. K. B. R. A. S. Vol. VIII, pp. 1–41. Seoul: 1917.

NOTES

1. *Aryavarman*, a man of Sinlo (*Corea*), left Chang'an A.D. 638. He set out with a view to recover the true teaching and to adore the sacred relics. He dwelt in the Nalanda Temple, copying out many Sutras. He had left the eastern borders of Corea and now bathed in the Dragon pool of Nalanda. Here he died, aged seventy odd years.

Hwui-nieh, a Corean, set out for India 638 A.D., arrived at the Nalanda Temple and there studied the sacred books and reverenced the holy traces. I-tsing found some writing he had left in the temple, where also he had left his Sanskrit MSS. The priests said he died the same year, about sixty years of age.

Hiuen Ta'i, a doctor of the law, a Corean, called by the Sanskrit name of Sarvajñanadeva. In the year *Yung-hwei* (650 A.D.) he went by the Tibetan road through Nepal to Mid-India; he there worshipped the relics at the Bodhi Tree. Afterwards going to the Tukhara country, he met Taou-hi, with whom he returned to the Tahsio Temple (Mahabodhi). Afterwards he returned to China, and was not heard of again.

Hiuen-hau, a doctor of the law, a Corean, went with Hiuen-chiu, in the middle of the *Chengkwan* period, to India, and reaching the Tahsio Temple, he died there.

Two priests of Corea, names unknown, started from Chang'an by the southern sea-route and came to Sribhoja. They died in the country of *Po-lu-sse,* to the westward (the western portion of Sumatra).

NOTES

Hwui Lun, a Corean, otherwise called Prajñavarma, came by sea from his own country to *Fuchau,* and proceeded thence to Chang'an. Following after the priest *Hiuen-chiu,* he reached the West, and during ten years dwelt in the Amravat country and in the Sin-ché Temple (north of the Ganges). Passing through the eastern frontiers, and thence proceeding northward he came to the Tu-ho-lo (*Tukhâra*) Temple. Beal: *Life of Hiouen-Tsiang,* pp. xxix–xxx, xxxvi.

2. Jones in his admirable discussion of the Eunjin miriok makes an interesting suggestion regarding its location:

> But the special interest these facts have for us in connection with the great Buddha lies in the fact that it may have been here that Buddhism itself first entered Pakche. Buddhism was a foreign importation, being sent to the peninsular kingdoms by the Eastern Tsin dynasty of China (A.D. 317–19) and effecting an entrance almost simultaneously at two points — in the north into Koguryu and in the south into Pakche. Of this latter event the native historians tell us: — "In the year A.D. 384 the barbarian monk Maranant'a came from Tsin. King Chip-yu accorded him a most courteous and ceremonious reception and Buddhism was established as the national religion." We do not know at what point the monk-missionary landed, but it is not so unlikely that he may have come to this well-known port, and that one day among the ships making up that inextricable mass of masts and rudders at Si-jin there may have come the imperial junk of Tsin bearing " the barbarian monk Maranant'a " with his images, incense, bells, books and vestments to plant in Korea that cult which was to dominate the

people for a thousand years, thus landing close to the place where in later years the greatest monument that Buddhism possesses was to stand. And two hundred years later (A.D. 552) there probably embarked from this port that band of Pakche priests sent by their king to carry to the mikado of Japan the golden images of Buddha and the triad of precious ones, the sutras and sacred books, and to give the faith of Buddhism to the Sun-rise Empire. And it is said that these relics exist to this day and are preserved in the city of Nagano in Japan. Colossal Buddha: p. 62.

3. It occurs in the inscription regarding the Seoul pagoda and is particularly interesting as a contemporary description of a temple of remarkable splendor.

Reckoning up the number of pillars supporting the building they were found to exceed 300. The Hall of the Buddha stood up high in the center, and the inscription board above was written *Taikwang myung jun*, "Great light glorious palace." To the left was the *Sun Tang* or study hall, while to the right was the *Oon-chip* or assembly hall. The gate was marked *Chakkwang Moon*, Hidden Light and the outer gate was called *Panya* or Likeness gate. Beyond this again was the *Hai-tal Moon*. There was a bell-pavilion also which was called the *Pup-noi-kak*, Kiosk of Buddha's Thunder. The kitchen was named *Hyang-juk*, Kitchen House. There was a pond on the east side, where lotus flowers were planted; and on the west was a garden-park where flowers and trees grew. Behind the *Cheung-jun* palace the sacred books were in keeping, and this house was called *Hai-Jang Chun* or Sea Covering Hall. Also a pagoda was built of thirteen stories called

NOTES

sul-to-pa, Buddhist pagoda. Within it were placed
the accumulated sari and the newly translated
Wun-gak sutra. The palaces, halls, studies, guest-
rooms, stores, kitchens, outhouses, had each their
particular place. The whole was magnificent
and well constructed, and the ornaments were
lavish, imposing, beautiful, all in keeping and
fair to see. Its equal was nowhere to be found.
Also the drums, gongs, etc., necessary for the
service, and other useful implements were abun-
dantly provided for. Gale: *Pagoda,* p. 10.

4. Gale finds that the history of the erection of the
Seoul pagoda was originally inscribed upon the turtle-
borne slab that accompanies it. Of the pagoda itself,
he says:

1. The Pagoda was therefore built in 1464–
1466 A.D.

2. The builder was King Se-jo, who reigned
from 1456–1468 and all the workmen were
Koreans.

3. The form of it was modelled after the
Pagoda in Pung Tuk County, which had already
been standing nearly a hundred years, and had
been built by Chinese workmen. There is no
evidence that this pagoda had ever been brought
from Peking though it finds its final resting
place now in Tokyo.

4. It was built to commemorate the excellence
of the Wungak Sutra from which it takes its
name.

5. It is by far the most interesting Buddhist
monument in Korea. p. 22.

5. The list of the thirty head-temples follows:

Yongju-sa   Chŭntung-sa
Pongeum-sa   Pongsŭm-sa

Makok-sa	Unhă-sa
Pawpchu-sa	Koun-sa
Songkwang-sa	Kumyong-sa
Sŭnam-sa	Peyak-sa
Tĕhung-sa	Sawngpul-sa
Păkyang-sa	Yungmyung-sa
Uipong-sa	Pawphung-sa
Posawk-sa	Pohyun-sa
Tongdo-sa	Kŭnpong-sa
Pomo-sa	Yuchom-sa
Hăin-sa	Ualchung-sa
Tonghwa-sa	Sawkwang-sa
Chuim-sa	Kuichu-sa

6. The magazine conducted by Yi Nung Hwa has had several breaks in publication and after each the name has been changed. As here given the names are English translations of the original:

Monthly Magazine of Chosen Buddhism. Nineteen issues, from January 25, 1911 to August 25, 1913.

Buddhist Magazine of the Eastern Sea. Eight issues from November 20, 1913 to June 20, 1914.

Monthly Magazine of the Association of Rising Buddhism. Nine issues from March 15, 1915 to December 15, 1915.

Kingdom of Chosen Buddhism. Three issues from April 5, 1916 to June 5, 1916.

General Magazine of Chosen Buddhism, from March 20, 1917. Three numbers had appeared when I received this note in May 1917.

7. The texts most commonly read in Korean monasteries are the *Hokkekyo, Kegon, Kishinlon, Fumonbon* and *Amidakyo,* according to Madame Gordon. These are Japanese pronunciation.

8. The Japanese names of the four guardians are:
   Bishamon: east; blue; tower.
   Komoku: south; red; jewel.
   Jikoku: west; green; lute.
   Zocho: north; flesh; sword.

9. Three Buddhas have preceded Sakyamuni in the present *kalpa* and one is still to come before the *kalpa* ends. The entire list is:
   Krakuchanda (Pali, *Kakusanda*), "who solves doubt."
   Kanakamuni (P. *Konagamana*) "body radiant as gold."
   Kasyapa (P. *Kassapa*) "swallower of light."
   Sakyamuni.
   Maitreya. Legge: Fa-hien, p. 51.

10. The eight scenes in the Life of Buddha are:
   (*a*) Incarnation.
   (*b*) Birth.
   (*c*) Encounter with age, sickness, death.
   (*d*) Escape — with aid of the four heavenly kings.
   (*e*) Asceticism.
   (*f*) Enlightenment.
   (*g*) Preaching — "turning the wheel."
   (*h*) Nirvana.

Buddhism